AF488403

# ALL MOMS WORK

## BY
## KATE GREMILLION ROSENOW

ISBN: 979-8-9860726-0-9 (Paperback)
        979-8-9860726-1-6 (Hardback)
        979-9860726-2-3 (Ebook)

*This book is dedicated to the boys who made me a mom,
Harry and Cam, and all the wonderful moms in my life,
especially my mom Nanette.*

OUR MOMS DO SO MANY THINGS.
IT'S EASY TO SEE.

EACH ONE DOES IMPORTANT WORK,
BUT MAYBE
JUST A LITTLE DIFFERENTLY.

SOME MOMS WORK IN AN OFFICE
ON THEIR COMPUTERS
AND PHONES.

SOME MOMS ARE THE BOSS
IN CHARGE AND
RUN A BUSINESS THEY OWN.

SOME MOMS WORK AROUND THE HOUSE CLEANING MESSES AND FIXING TOYS.

SOME MOMS RUN ERRANDS
AND CARPOOL FOR
THEIR LITTLE GIRLS AND BOYS.

SOME MOMS VOLUNTEER
IN THE CLASSROOM
AND HELP OUT AT SCHOOL.

Aa
Bb
Cc

SOME MOMS WORK
IN GOVERNMENT
AND MAKE ALL THE LAWS
AND RULES.

SOME MOMS TRAVEL
FOR THEIR WORK
ON PLANES, TRAINS, AND CARS.

SOME MOMS TAKE US TO THE DOCTOR WHEN WE'VE HAD TOO MANY CHOCOLATE BARS.

SOME MOMS WORK IN
RESTAURANTS
AND MAKE FOOD
FOR ALL THE GUESTS.

SOME MOMS ARE CHEFS
AT HOME, AND THEIR MEALS ARE
SOME OF THE BEST.

SOME MOMS MAKE PRETTY THINGS
LIKE PAINTINGS, PICTURES,
AND CARDS.

SOME MOMS HELP US
DO OUR CHORES WHEN
THEY FEEL A BIT TOO HARD.

SOME MOMS GO TO COLLEGE
SO THEY CAN
LEARN AND EARN A DEGREE.

THEY STUDY, READ AND TAKE TESTS
AND STILL HELP YOU AND ME.

NO MATTER THE JOB DESCRIPTION
OR EXACTLY
WHAT TASKS THEY DO.

TO-DO

ALL MOMS ARE WORKING MOMS,
AND WE'RE THANKFUL
FOR ALL YOU DO.

# DRAW YOUR WORKING MOM

If you want, you can take a picture of your drawing and share it with us!
Tag us at @workwellwithkate or #AllMomsWork